All Beautiful Things Need Not Fly

spirit wheels
in tapestry of sky,
a white stitch between one life
and another.

(excerpt from "White Stitch" pg. 18)

All Beautiful Things Need Not Fly

All Beautiful Things Need Not Fly

Martin Willitts Jr.

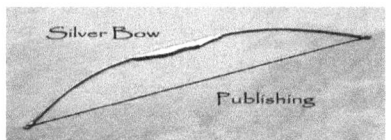

720 – Sixth Street, Box # 5
New Westminster, BC
V3C 3C5   CANADA

Title: All Beautiful Things Need Not Fly
Author: Martin Willitts Jr.
Publisher: Silver Bow Publishing
Cover Art: "The Love Birds" painting by Candice James
Layout/Design/Editing: Candice James
ISBN: 978-1-77403- 299-2 paperback
ISBN: 978-1-77403- 300-5 e- book

All rights reserved including the right to reproduce or translate this book or any portions thereof, in any form without the permission of the publisher. Except for the use of short passages for review purposes, no part of this book may be reproduced, in part or in whole, or transmitted in any form or by any means, either by means electronically or mechanically, including photocopying, recording, or any information or storage retrieval system without prior permission in writing from the publisher.

© Silver Bow Publishing 2024

Library and Archives Canada Cataloguing in Publication

Title: All beautiful things need not fly / Martin Willitts Jr.
Names: Willitts, Martin, Jr., author.
Identifiers: Canadiana (print) 20240332148 | Canadiana (ebook) 20240332172 | ISBN 9781774032992
  (softcover) | ISBN 9781774033005 (Kindle)
Subjects: LCGFT: Poetry.
Classification: LCC PS3623.I4769 A79 2024 | DDC 811/.54—dc23

All Beautiful Things Need Not Fly

To my wife, Linda Griggs

All Beautiful Things Need Not Fly

Contents

I

The Mountain Quail / 11
Work Horse / 12
Four Blue Horses / 13
Released From My Heart / 14
Searching For What We Will Never Find / 15
Burying Beetle / 16
Nothing Remains Perfectly Still / 17
A White Stitch / 18
After a Rough Season / 19
Shooting the Last Female White Giraffe / 20
Eastern Tiger Swallowtail / 21
Transitioning / 22
Reams of Light / 23
Blueberry Time / 24
Moon-Wave Manta Rays / 25
Blue Winged Darter / 26
Presence / 27
The Crane Maiden / 28
On a Walk / 29

II

Loggerhead Shriek / 33
The Glass-Faced Deer / 34
Dutchman's Breeches / 35
Crickets / 36
A Cricket / 37
The Frantic Calling / 38
Cows Have Their Own Language / 39
A Brief Encounter / 40
Canadian Geese / 42
Finding a Turtle / 43
A Startle of Monarchs / 44
Encounter / 45

A Flamingo Always Has One Leg Up
    Ready to Fly If It Needs To / 46
When Geese Leave / 47
The Elephants Sing About Everlasting Love / 48

III

Message / 51
A Drowning of Whales / 52
Against All Odds / 59
Why the Cicadas Are Noisy / 61
Dragonfly / 62
Awestruck / 64
Deer Country / 65
Today, My Voice is Full of Magpies / 66
Sky Writing / 67
Perfect and Terrifying / 68
Black-Capped Chickadee / 69
The Bird Count / 70
Grackles in Snow / 71
Light Entering / 72
Hawk Flight Before Snowfall / 73
Departing / 74
Red-Winged Blackbirds / 75

IV

The Mind Is an Eraser / 79
It Is All Written in Celtic Woods / 88
Our Hearts Are Weighed When We Are Born / 95

Acknowledgments / 103
Author Profile / 105

All Beautiful Things Need Not Fly

I

All Beautiful Things Need Not Fly

The Mountain Quail

It takes three years to hatch one egg.
Never reliable producers,
their hatchlings pop out, willy-nilly,
without any presentation
or poking or cracking.

You cannot tell between sexes,
and neither can they.
They all wear crests
of two black feathers,
causing no end of confusion.

Perhaps, they don't care,
slipping in and out of nests,
changing partners like at a dance,
patterns endlessly blurring,
accidental pairings of same sex
or not. Perhaps, it doesn't matter.

What I remember most is a coloring book
with an indistinguishable quail
leading five androgynous chicks
in a colorless field.
I wanted to give them a squiggle
of multi-color, go outside the borders,
splash them with every crayon,
confuse them into thinking
they were rushed hues.

I understood their care-free
nonchalance about mating.
Even at five, I knew my uncle
wore a dress, lipstick, rouge.

Life will not be so bland and monochrome.

Work Horse

Over the plain and simple Amish landscape,
they trot at a reasonable pace, nostrils
remembering when the air was clear,
clicking horseshoes on pavement or stone,
       sameness and repetitiveness,
         direction to and from
harsh white-quiet simple meetinghouse.

A simple tug on the reins, we'd be off.
They'd nicker about the workload.

I might pull with them to dislodge the wagon
grinding mud, or replace their shoes,
       or cool them off,
telling them sweet stories about endless fields
of buttercups and black flies that never bit.

They'd shake their heads, disagreeing,
recognizing my outrageous lies.
They know me all too well.

This world brings miles of disappointment,
      same forward and back.

Four Blue Horses
(Painting by Franz Marc)

the unseen out there
        rustles

these horses have been to the river
traces of loss on their muzzles

      water
colorless as sky

before darkness comes in
a herd grazing silence

rivers make statements
manes running wind-wild

      heads turn
to sounds we do not hear

     edge nearer
a river clip-clopping over stones

            neighing and striking
            forelocks on fall ground

                  a storm gallops
                  cloud hoofprints

Released from My Heart

through last glaze of clouds
    geese return

slender in distance
their calling reaches before they do

some patterns never change
twenty pounds of anxiety releases from a heart

we think we know every experience
      we do not

we need to change our patterns
returning to longing for better than this

Searching for What We Never Find

a long white shadow of a stork
crosses the pea-green algae pond

testing for cool water
focusing on the grassy surface

      questions distort
        what is real

        what is not
        does it matter

light passes through a white clapboard house
          a ricocheting bird
    tries to get out a closed window

Burying Beetle

A black beetle with red markings
on its forewings emerges
from inside the carcass of a bird.

I forget how we are all hosts to something else.
We all feed; taking in the spirit of the dead
so we can survive, then something feasts on us.

Some say this is ghoulish, but this is life
and death: the recycling of existence.
And it is messy; life is never neat and pretty.

Some ask where God is in all of this?
We want to bury truth, pretend there is more
than larva and decomposition.

We want to compose a reality in stanzas,
a lyric beauty worthy of stature and dignity.

    It is impossible.

God's grand design is huge.
Questioning is what we do best.
A burying beetle does what it does best.

Nothing Remains Perfectly Still

Turbulence was unexpected.
A mallard's brood went into ocean crest and tremor.

    Ducks had entered single file,
yellow round notes on a music sheet.

    At first, they rocked gently
in white foam, contentedly quaking.

A shift of intent, then waves thrashed heavily,
    an orchestra rushing to finish.

    The ducklings disappeared
under a large, curling drum roll wave,

    bobbed up like corks
from after-shocks, cymbal thrashed under.

My heart crests and tremors
    these turbulences.

A White Stitch

A whooping crane, rising
from molecules of a lake,
    impacts silence —
all noticeable objects reflect
and amplify noise. Commotion
becomes crystal and shatters.

      Not flight,
not suddenness emerging out of water,
    but the troubling way
 spirit comes out of nowhere —

        spirit wheels
     in tapestry of sky,
  a white stitch between one life
      and another.

A tall, languishing of white with red crest
comes into existence —
a struggling sound leaving
the bellows of its lungs to its long neck,
straining over centuries to reach its release,
calling the others into unison.

    Others join.

    Morning arrives,
in the raised mound of a marsh-edge,

I find two olive-colored eggs.

  Statistically,
only one will make it.

After a Rough Season

ducks lift together into a bravo clap
        sound tumbling
    across the green marsh

each day outstretching arms take us in
        settle us down
        loose feathers

        seasons pace in our mind
          anxious to get going
           sound mirroring
      across marsh water surface
           dappling rain
      concentric hypnotic wrinkles

ducks skate across the pond
        ripping water

we continue to tear pieces of the bad days
until whatever we thought was true
           vanishes

        seasons close in on us
a clatter of ducks sweeping over a pond

Shooting the Last Female White Giraffe

It has come to this:
every wrong decision
becomes someone else's mistake.

We need to resolve whatever we can.
We cannot let the world get set so far back
it appears intractable, beyond re-setting.

We have to be sensitive to have common sense.

Already, polar ice caps have retreated,
      exposing bare rock.

We should have suspected negative consequences
when we tracked the dodo into non-existence.

Once, the sky was blackened
by carrier pigeons, and forests crowded
out the light. Once, we practiced the love
we preached and summoned our decency.

      Everything has led to this:

      we consider it a triumph
      if we live through each day.

We've turned the corner, turned our backs
when Adam and Eve, cast out of Eden,
never glanced back, learning why bother
preserving what you can't ever keep.

Eastern Tiger Swallowtail Larvae on Black Cherry Tree

Survival is always precarious.
Parts disconnect, multiple-life forms fail.
Many situations can go wrong in life. They often do.

A male tiger swallowtail with
orange and blue spots near its tail,
traces an indirect route
to a milkweed near the vacant road.
Survival depends on feasting and hosting.

Female tiger swallowtails lay their eggs
on Black Cherry leaves,
furthest from their natural enemies.
Survival depends on good choices.

When their eggs hatch, the larvae look like bird droppings.
This camouflage will protect them more than prayer,
more than luck, more than distance and closeness
to their enemies. Survival depends on camouflage.

Growing to caterpillars, they turn as green
as a Black Cherry leaf, responding to that deep calling
of survival, a song in their green bloodstream.

They have a resting stage when transformation begins
in their greenish-brown chrysalis, small as a thumb.
If the weather turns unexpectedly cold,
these butterflies might wait for spring to emerge.

Those bright eyespots on their wings are not true eyes.
Their illusions scare their predators
or make predators attack the wrong part.
Survival depends on patience.

Transitioning

flight babbles its presence
its restless efforts to amaze and amuse
knowing it only lasts for a brief summer

      a mere sampling of milkweed

all good moments are always arriving
a language of butterfly movements

words ebb out into night
   purpling the sky

Reams of Light

herons take off
wrinkled white sheets

stirring ancient machinery
a haunting sound

I find abandoned nests

    drawers
empty of silverware

Blueberry Time

Bees stroke blueberry blossoms,
patching light inside each pestle and stamen,
content with their simple job of transforming flowers
into berries, humming love songs while taking pollen,
packing dreams inside each flower,
brushing some hint of music.

Bees begin their choreographed dances, their magic
of time and pollination until blueberries appear:
first white, then light red to royal dark-blue,
standing in rain, heat, and star-wink.

Moon-Wave Manta Rays

Rays move inky waters,
an excited student knowing the answer.

Their devil-may-care bodies seem to yawn,
feeling silky water handling them.

Rays skitter across the ocean floor,
skipping to a made-up song.

Blue-Winged Darter (Dragonfly)

There was a time when he wasn't,
    when he floated,
      a larva
   about to be named,
  making music from one
quicksilver stage to another.

      He crawled
out of clear, motionless water
  shredding his papery skin.

He'd skim-skirt
a shear wetland surface,
generating noise
with metallic bluish-white wings,
zipping a singular, repeating,
elongating note,
shimmering hum,
as soft as the left behind shell,

     a transient,
    from place
  to contemplative place
      to exit,
to a stronger, flamboyant finish.

Presence

cranes lift their sudden heads
from shinning
　　　crystalline
　　　　water surface
　　　　soaked with rain

raise vertically
　　over
white spruce

　　take off
into concave wind
opening a window lattice

　　leaving
shuddering branches
　　damp grass
　their absence

The Crane Maiden
Three haiku based on the Japanese fairy tale

*

the girl's hands move slow
feathers on the loom and air,
neck bent to weaving

*

she weaves soft whiteness —
origami snow-white cranes,
small boned birds in flight

*

I open her door —
a startle of snow feathers,
silence of branches

*

cranes pass through moonglow
twist white after-images
shapes of cranes remain

On a Walk

A snowy owl in his white cotton-bathrobe
ruffles his wings, then settles back,
a cranky old man. Whatever he thinks
he hears, twitches his ear.

All Beautiful Things Need Not Fly

All Beautiful Things Need Not Fly

II

All Beautiful Things Need Not Fly

Loggerhead Shriek

Sing me a song of knives,
sharp skies cutting shadows into prey
you impale on thorn branches. Sing
thralls of death and screeching for mercy,
giving none, hanging your victim
like a butcher hooks a slab.

This song becomes
as frequent as a hot sunrise of locust wings.
A kind of sonogram hearing no heartbeat.
Your lack of a talon doesn't stand in your way.

You bring appointments of death,
bits of gnashes, edible chunks flaying,
blood in the beak of a moon.

        We call you butcherbird,
        you bring bereavement.

You are deceptive; small as a robin,
but blood-thirsty, savage, offering finality.
Sing me a memorial, a surge of loss.
Perch your disproportionate head
with its judge and jury outlook,
whistling like a hangman.

Your tune is a guillotine.
Your face wears a black hood.
Eyes watch for begging
before proceeding. A scale of justice
weighs less than you and your song,
an unmusical tune, not in pitch, not planned,
pure thoughtfulness. A repeated *tink,*
clapping of brutal metal,
grinding of axes,
piercing of a prey
on rusty barbed wire.

The Glass-Faced Deer

They rope it from a snowmobile,
      brand it,
         cage it
for a Christmas display
in bulletproof glass.

Children ask if it can fly.

Someone lets the deer loose.
It breaks into a grocery store,
eating carrots and wild blueberries.

      It runs
  as the moon runs
behind clouds and migrating geese,
      followed by
an angry pack of snowmobiles
leaping over snow banks
      like deer.

Dutchman's Breeches

I follow bumblebees through early Illinois spring
to turned-down white flowers.
Sometimes, unplanned moments are best.

I get lost, wandering like this,
in the strangeness of bee flight.
I do not care.

I don't see clearly until I am lost.
Perhaps, the lack of caring led me to this:
burrs stick to my pants. Thistles rack my hands.

Sometimes, you have to let life just happen
in order to find out what is important.
I follow the bees to this special place

in their own indirect way. Here I am,
not in any hurry to get back,
near these flowers that look like pants.

Dutchman's breeches only last a week or two.
They depend on the bees for their brief survival.
I stare at them with the many eyes of bees.

Crickets

While planting thick, miniature, devilish gardens
of leopard-spotted ferns, there, in humbling silence,
an almost-sound our ears have almost forgotten.
We almost missed the crickets' faint beginnings.
It takes a while for recognition to plant itself,
a secret we almost missed.

        A cricket sings thanks.

As summer heat grows fierce as penance,
the cricket sings sharper and faster.
We can measure heat by its frantic clicking,
when everything cools, it slows its message.
Songs carry dawn throughout night
as if its songs of praise are never long enough.

And after all, isn't it what this is really all about?
This singing life, this tremble of heart and heat,
chants of simple pleasures. These sublime desires,
hiding in greenness with incredibly grateful singing.

The Cricket

A cricket preaches in song.
It has one short season
to serenade the green as a lover.

When summer is gone, a tiny silence
afterwards becomes the loss all lovers feel
       when love leaves.

I am singing too, my last song,
notes of green leaves,
under an open window of moonlight.

      Night hears me,
knows my bamboo-flute heart. knows
shortening seasons.

Music in vines, intertwine around each other —
    lovers, making cricket-noises,
surrendering to the coda of the moment.

The Frantic Calling

The bluish butterfly bush calls to me —
its nectar to taste, mash against my nose,
summer spring-mist for my hair.
I want to swim in it. Have its stickiness on my arms.
Want to be heavy with slumber and fullness,
drunk with honey, slid my tongue in, a spoon,
flute it to get the most of it, uncoil it into my belly.
Then who would question if I sprouted feelers,
papery wings of symmetrical spots emerged,
and I migrated to Mexico and back?
The honey locust tree would be next.

This brutal elegance of waiting
    becomes impossible,
blossoms of music almost heard
from behind my locked white doors.

Cows Have Their Own Sense of Time

Cows follow light-years behind us,
all hush and calm, heartbeats of prayers,
while the universe shifts into high gear.

When the barn calls to them at night,
they lift bent heads; ears tune like antennas.

No wonder Georgia O'Keeffe picked up a cow's skull
to peer into one eye hole at the blue sky,
to hear echoes of life and death, then
fetched paint brushes with bristles
soft as the tip of a cow's tail.

>I ask grandfather,
>*what are the cows saying?*

Grandfather does not seem to know,
or if he does, he doesn't say.

>Where the cows stand,
>suns spiral in galaxies.

A Brief Encounter

A grasshopper lands on my palm,
idles in one place, until I notice a tingling.
He sketches words onto the page of my skin.

The grasshopper felt blades of grass,
dew dissolving like promises
from morning sun, and smooth stones
that held the keepsake of coldness for ages
before anyone was born.

      The grasshopper stays
like a person pulling over to see a mountain view,
gazing at the endless possibilities of sky
and clouds, wondering what to notice next.

And what does the grasshopper think of me?

I want silence to hear what he needs to say,
his green jaws moving wind in grass.

I can't say if he regards me as a curiosity
with his complex eyes; or if rubbing his back legs
on his front, generating stridulations, is for me
or a female grasshopper: or if I am jumping to conclusions.

Its wings, gentle as eyelashes, begin to twitch,
acting as if it is beyond time to go,
to leap vigorously into a new adventure.

For a moment, stillness lasts forever.
      This world touches me.

I don't need a church to understand
what a complex world this can be,
or how the urge to kneel in the presence of light
pulls its invisible rope, dragging me,
kicking and screaming, or gently.

All Beautiful Things Need Not Fly

I don't need more time, more silence,
to know my soul is moved by a sudden breeze.

My soul might be a red bird
that is not a cardinal, in the understated heavens,
sharing a song with that grasshopper
about this astonishing world —

opens us up more; closes us up more.

Canadian Geese

Their noisy beginnings, stretching the sky,
interminable returns,

come & depart in right angles, almost taking treetops off,
wedging into a last echoed song.

This ritual happens twice yearly, never the same, never
changing, always knowing when change is coming.

> They remember what we forget:
> this world is the same & different,
> always in flight, always nesting,
>
> we cannot lift out of our bodies,
> nor see the land slowly below us,
> nor call the changing of the seasons
> so it will change like they can.

This is how love begins: the calling & responding.
This is how we should migrate & mate, and dip into water,

taking turns leading & following so neither of them tires,
in a formation of co-operation so none are left behind.

Finding a Turtle

                I tell my son
terrapin shells hold the secret to Teutonic plates —
he thinks: dinner plates with painted peonies.

          The box turtle nudges
              across a stream
of endless stars, like smooth dull stones.

The turtle tugs its prehistoric head into its shell
like a person afraid to admit the truth:
this earth is plodding to extinction.

My son asks, what if the plates pull apart,
will we fall in the cracks?
He remembers how dinner plates break.

He requests to take the turtle home.
He'd seen one smashed by tires.
I say it belongs here in the wild.

He considers fragile peonies,
stars drowning in silence,
trash piling with nowhere to go.

He suggests the turtle is safer with us.
He dwells on fissures of life and death.
He demands a turtle shell for a body.

A Startle of Monarchs

Abundance departed
in a single motion,
monarchs blending
into fields of milkweed —
startling dogwoods into bloom again
and again
and again.

Miles of sacredness
go into a world that never lasts.

Encounter

A horse was heaving
after almost running out of its skin,
trying to leave this world
breathlessly behind.

There are moments like this —

perfect surrender — never lasting.
Some of us catch a glimpse of it,
a tail flickering light.

Rising out of our darkness,
          love rises,
   merging with twilight.

A horse throws itself into that moment,
     leaves its old self behind.

All Beautiful Things Need Not Fly

A Flamingo Always Has One Leg Up, Ready to Fly If It Needs To

the weight of life trembles down night
shaking curtains made out of rocks

a blink un-does this world
fumbles with the way-it-used-to-be

        overhead

near-perfect rain breaks the heat

    life turns quiet without you

        rain writes this down

When Geese Leave

When geese leave, I ask them,
please take me with you.

I'm convinced they are going elsewhere —
a place of many secrets.

I want that out-of-body experience;
not to be earthbound, left behind.

The Elephants Sing About Everlasting Love

We are blessed, sing the elephants,
but our world is in trouble and distress.
The earth has too much damage;
we feel the land's sadness through our feet
as we travel in a herd towards polluted rivers.

    Something is amiss.

We change our songs yearly,
discovering new destruction,
hearing keening from the soil.

We sing, nevertheless, across the horizon
to where the land descends into wretchedness.

The way we respect the dead lasts generations —
an unending music of legacy and respect.

    We remember.

We honor the bones
of our ancestors with the same joyful caring
for the land and the air, sharing our chorus
with those who have no reason to sing.

    We are blessed.

The dirt we toss on our backs
is blessed. The savanna and the shrub trees
providing leaves to eat are blessed. The sun
watching over us is blessed.
The water we drink with blessedness
sprays over us to consecrate ourselves
in the survey of all that we see. A water
contains the spirit of every song ever sung,
every refrain wanting to be shared.

All Beautiful Things Need Not Fly

III

All Beautiful Things Need Not Fly

Message

Ascending flat needles on the balsam fir,
loose, irregular, feathery needles of the hemlock,
shaggy leaves of the cottonwood
and flat sprays of northern white cedar,
        are all I can see.

If something were to happen to me,
taken away from all of this,
the forest would remain
long after I was gone.

        I know I am going soon.
I hear it from the yellow warbler hanging in branches
of Lombard poplar. Its crisp music remains there,
slender in those continuous branches.

The warbler flies into tomorrow
    taking news to others —

    they will be leaving too.

The Drowning of Whales

1.

Whales beach themselves in clusters,
      singing their dying,
waves of intense suffering and surrender,
      not unlike our own.

Their out-of-body song stretches across sand
as an offering: a hymn of things from the past,
the long journey through dark waters
into the future, where we will all swim
in meteor showers, common as folk songs,
forgotten as the passing of ages
hidden within the circle of a tree stump.

      O, their terrible singing.

They breathe sighs of night-songs,
surface, breaking through air,
shattering breath into sandy crystals,
into angels or fishermen lost at sea.

2.

Multiple whales beach themselves,
following the calling of others, that same sound
we all hear before we, too, die,
whooshing out breath with seashells, barnacles,
lost chances, low tides in our ebbing.

In that last flash of belly-song,
our bodies shutter along with the whales.

Ours is a song of coming and going.
We surface into currents, into the winds,
into the swells — wherever songs take us.

Some already dive into the deepest waters of death
while their graying bodies remained landlocked,
    swimming from nothingness
into light, into that final song, into whale-fall.

3.

We swim because we must,
towards our own calling.
Float towards our final coastline.

4.

Whales sing their final sonata:
a joyful hymn from a ship's pump organ.
Bellows from bottomless sighs.

Whales are joined on the beach by other whales.
They die in spite of our best efforts.

We rub their bodies with water,
keeping them hydrated
for as long as they can take the suffering.
Then we remember *that* fear
pulling at us with final tides —

that fear of being on life support:
a hospital hydrating us
in our shell, within our longing,
within our beached bodies,
within endless beaches of our silence.

We would not want to continue on life support.
We would want that final diving
into sound beyond the barrier reefs,
jellyfish rotating as spiral constellations.

5.

      Whales open their mouths,
wide caves of dark intensity and mystery.

They swim in pods. In family groups so close,
they are more than families.
Whale text messages are sounds
strung through the ocean, connecting them
in ways we could never understand.

For when one whale gets in trouble,
they all get in trouble. They all share
the same fate. They all share the same risks.

Whales are, in many ways, more civilized than us,
communicating through song,
sharing the same melody,
moving within music as if it was water.

Some people have seen other people suffer
and do nothing, seen people shot or watched hunger,
never lifting a finger to do anything.
Whale-calling clings to us with dampest fog.

6.

There was a scientist who studied beached whales.
He hypothesized when cool Antarctic waters,
drenched in squid, flow north, whales pursue the water
        towards the edge of land;

or perhaps, killer whales panic other whales,
herding them towards the shoreline.

I rub the whale's strange rubbery skin with water.
        Its life depends upon it.
Tidal flow brought this adversarial situation.
Shallowness and slope of land became death traps.

Whales slow singing — each voice
    ebbing away into silence.

Music echoes from whale to whale,
as death-watch continues into night.
Already, distinct keening from terns.
    Waterline of memory.

Night's memoriam. Laps edges of dreams.
Final lights osculate, leading the way.

7.

We all become well-versed in this final music.
We move in currents of our own calling:
from whale bone to angle of light,
wheeling birds in the chorus.

Bulkiness of this song makes awkwardness.
Lean against the music and push.
The whale refuses to move,
conceding itself to clumsiness
and unwieldiness of inert motion,
allowing to drift out of itself.

8.

I once held a hand of a person
as they parted seas of darkness,
felt light leaving their body,
swimming into the beyond,
until only memory remained.

There are so many things we do not know.
This lack of understanding
is massive as a dying whale.

Whale soundings from depths sang volumes.

Something we can never understand
until too late, until we, too, experience dying.

      Immensity of life,
        largeness of the ocean,
        swimming towards light —
      these are all we can know.

The skin-and-bone simplicity
   of whales singing,
rejoicing what we will hear,
confessions we have ignored.

The spontaneous singing is electric,
spindling out of ourselves,
a part of the spindle of life.

9.

We can be sober in music,
or lash ourselves in the gales.
We can push against
this solemn body of requiems,
or feel melody humming inside.

Sooner or later, we all give up.
We give into that somniferous sound
prompting us into the next chapter.

We will move in unison to that music:

whether stridulating of insects,
or rudeness of woodpeckers
boring a hole into the sky,
or the refrain from the last drenching rain.

10.

Their last breath whistles.

We feel ourselves whine.
A thickness of silence.
Wind grates against our numbness,
sets our teeth on edge.

There is an exclamation following the silence.
A collective awe, almost unexpected.
We ebb with tides. A harmony inside us,
an ocean breeze from a blowhole,
a recognition we cannot explain.

A measure within us, a music measure,
a beat we must follow —
trailing after a school of fish.
Our final aria, a duet with the world around us,
we have to sing.

We are in the presence of Silence.

11.

A flash flush with meteorites, of deep
undercurrent, deeper than
most of us have ever been —

quietude drenches the sea-body
with weightless notes:
forgiveness and memory
pulsates on the shore,
an infrequent heartbeat
before dying as a last star.

12.

In God-light, none of us are truly adrift.
We are numbered easily among
many grains of nameless sand.

Stars appear to be motionless.
They are not.
Not any more than we are.

13.

We move away from the whale.

Reporters ask questions none can answer.
Silence, unspoken, looms in turbulent sky.
Nothing can save the whales.

    In crests of waves
we find light from the first star
    before heading back
        into the deep.

Against All Odds

Every year, I give the forsythia a haircut —
    a little off the top —

a toad has taken up residence under it.
I haven't seen it lately, though.
What are the odds of seeing it again?

And this is the year
against the odds of survival,
locusts return, breaking the silence,
overwhelming the area
with their boisterous chatter —

    their frenzied sex —
   twenty feet out of reach.

I clip the forsythia to no avail.
I snip, yet can't keep up with their growth —
the bush has other plans —

the odds are stacked against me —
an explosion of stems and flower tips.

I would ask advice from the toad —
assuming he's at home, hiding from me
like a tenant avoiding a rent-due bill —

but I cannot hear him if he's there
over the racket of the locusts,
hundreds of chainsaws.

There is much I cannot see in this world,
    like the locusts
pressing the issue of their existence
    or the toad, laying low,
   trying to be inconspicuous.

All Beautiful Things Need Not Fly

Some life I can see like the forsythia, jauntily
showing off. And then, there is me, trimming
fitfully between frustration and surrender
or continuing against all odds.

Why the Cicadas Are Noisy

My sister hears whirring voices
in a claustrophobic room, whispering about her.

Cicadas appear in thirteen-year cycles, loud
rapid buckling and unbuckling noises like tymbals.
Yet, my sister could care less about their music.
The world collapses around her head,
the buzzsaw of people yacking and clacking,
rusty and nail-bitingly annoying.

Cicada dwell inside of trees, living off sap,
laying their eggs inside slits between tree bark
with tiny internal messages on when to come alive.
My sister asks *what's the purpose of living*?
Hesitation marks on your wrist mark off attempts,
trails no one can follow to rescue her.

Cicadas wait for *Emergence*.
Her husband has hidden the knives.

Cicadas emerge at different times to fool any predator.
The therapist never sees the times
my sister appears distressed,
flung out of control, her only ease whole bottles of pills.
Her husband has hidden them where she can't find them,
then she discovers another method, more sneaky
than cicada cycles, confusing their predators.

The Greeks and Chinese believed cicadas were immortal.
Although my sister is not immortal,
she can try to live another day.
Just in case, her husband has hidden the knives.

Dragonfly

1.

Curl of sleep, intangibly beautiful —
an amber dragonfly glides about an inch
above pond-scum water,
demonstrating inevitable risk at temptation,

hovers at the same closeness as language
when words suddenly demand more attention.
The world's events remind us
tender moments and violence can co-exist.

   Currents of surprise stir
by blue wings of the dragonfly.

2.

The dragonfly writes its message in air:
this untraceable world is as fragile
as a paper lantern in a storm.

Many versions of this world
are necessary to fit in every image
a dragonfly sees.

3.

A half-moon — or locust shell —
on a cold, still night, empty,
      abandoned,
like a white porcelain dish,
observed up close and skimmed
      a blank page.

> The dragonfly
has no time for discernment
> or silent contemplation.

4.

A dragonfly twists in air,
making it wrinkle

> folding air
into a blue bed sheet.

The dragonfly becomes a haze,
beating in a singular noise —

> *hizzzzzzzzz,*
as silent as a shark.

5.

His body glows neon
> advertising
on where to find the best cattails
> or lily pads.

6.

A woman gets a dragonfly tattoo,
and it flies out of her skin.

7.

a dragonfly darts
> and darns
amber setting sunlight.

Awestruck

drumming clatter of geese
        head north
answering the call to return
breaking the boundaries of my heartbreak
loudly proclaiming their presence
crossing the invisible bridge of life
        and death

Deer County

I've seen night beating its frightened heart.
An apparition appears out of nowhere —

I should have gone slower at that time of night
when objects loom suddenly. A deer zig-zags.

We all should compensate for the unknown.
We never know what lurks in the dark.

Fear stokes more fear, jolting us,
a deer bolting out of the dark —

finding a tuff of brown hairs on a car
or lose a windshield or broken engine block.

On rain-slick roads, when deer lunge
like heart attacks. We pull over after a thud,

find nothing but a small dent we could beat out
with a ball peen hammer. Or find a deer

pulled to the side like a marker, red glass splinters
from a broken break light like blood splatter.

In a blink, every moment can change direction
and night takes your heart in its hand.

The unknown lurks in either light or dark.
We never see the inevitable coming.

If we could, we'd swerve,
sigh many heart-jerks, many tear-jerks.

Sometimes, we'd survive the deer combat zone.
Sometimes, we make it home in time, undented.

Today, My Voice is Full of Magpies

One magpie presents danger. See two,
there will be a marriage; see three,
a person is about to go on a journey;
see six, and there will be an ending;

nine will talk non-stop about love.
Always welcome a magpie nest,
for love will roost in our houses.
Magpies chase away false ideas, scolding them.

If they build a nest in the thickest split of a tree,
they build spiritual doorways. Enter.
Magpies are flamboyant, reminding us
we should never hide from the world.

There are times to become shy and reclusive
          as the magpie.
A gathering of magpies becomes a bridge:
      expect the unexpected.

Sky Writing

A gust of sparrows shakes the trees,
withdrawing and returning all day.
The language of settled days
thrashes awake, air kicking up,
ruffling, yanking light's threads,
tangling it among the branches,
clotheslines, and fences.

They never do finish
what they're determined to do

to be in the moment,
to be that moment,
gust-shaking trees,

writing, again
- and again,
- and
- again,

temporary messages.

Perfect and Terrifying

Raucous birdcalls cross the field,
creating turbulence in the upper branches,
shaking and quaking, rattling trees,
a few aftershocks, then

      quiet.

What caused the stir, what settled it?

Some hidden presence must have caused
this brief transference of power,
an immeasurable flux and tranquil resolve.

Maybe it was nothing, nothing at all —
just a momentary blast of uncertainty.
But once that sound stirred my heart,
it took a while to recover.

The birdcalls cease — quiet
turns more deafening, light diffuses,
    forest dampening
with queries as to what makes silence
    perfect and terrifying.

Black-Capped Chickadee

You may be the size of a whisper,
but I hear your pleas, your exaltations,
your design on the blueprint of the sky.

You do not abandon me, nor migrate.
You are faithful when many are not;
cheerful when others are downcast.

You make the sound of summer rain.
You warn or contact others
with discernment and abandonment.

Oh, if only I was this joyous —
knowing pleasure in every day assurances,
flittering in the music stanzas of branches,

my songs would fly into the stars,
into God's gracious arms, held,
mending my broken wing.

      Ah. If only.
I'd build a nest of truth.

          Please bird.
Tell me how to fly with such music.

The Bird Count

moving in night
among seedless
trees following tracks

blue shadows in snow
by a deserted train station
near a frozen lake

no open water
for kingfishers
we are the only sound

this desolate place
too cold for birds
clouds never lifted

their grey wings
covered with ice
we cannot see our hands

a cluster of cardinals
a dense field of red
on ashen ground

Grackles in Snow

In a murmur-storm,
line of sight
obliterates, thin shadows of trees,
no sign of where sleep ends and
when morning testifies
it is cold-time,

a rip in the sky,
an intruder, white snow
covers several counties
with a greyness, almost dark,

black notes of grackles land
on shaking-loose snow.

What will they find worth having?

In the carpet of white,
I brush snow off the car window,
scrape veneer of ice,
lift wiper blades to open
defrost slats
in blue-cold bitterness.

I have to unlearn shortages,
slightness of light,

improbable grackles never flinching,
short surprise of snow
landing and melting on my eyelashes.

Light Entering

Egrets follow cows in pastures,
white exclamation marks,
stick-figure shadows,

stilt-walkers,
a parade of white banners
in a straight line,
monks to a service.

Light enters even cow's milk,
common grass,
long necks of egrets,
still distances
yet to be explored.

Light passes through quiet stillness,
    music,
 white feathers before taking flight.

Hawk Flight before Snowfall

Downhill from jutted chins of outcrop rocks,
weather rubs its troubled hands of snow.

The ground heaves stone-cold breaths.
Snow grinds every breath into determined movement.

A weather-beaten fence remembers a red-tail hawk,
its slightest movements, its sharp, intense focus.

A mouse flattens in turbulent silence.
Hawk strikes, snatches.

Shadows and breath fly out of a heart,
gone before snow or judgment.

If I have lived only this long in the emptying wind,
then silence with its message can have its own deepness.

Departing

        when geese leave
they take what little is left of summer with them

    the rest of the world pauses as their calling dissolves
        water lapping at a river's edge

        silence afterwards
we are all aware what will happen next

tiny brown birds twittering in grasses
throwing their best songs at death

dark-grey snow clouds do not stop their freeze
tinging green leaves into shriveling and falling

each season of killing frost arrives earlier
our best songs are never good enough

we increase the odds of destruction
taking earth into oblivion where birds never sing

Red-Winged Blackbirds

Male blackbirds are the first to migrate,
locating the best nesting spots
before some other male. It has to be safe
with plenty of food. It has to be patrolled,

so, they fly the perimeter,
calling and puffing their red patches
for other males to see.

Brown-streaked females arrive later,
brides late for their own wedding,
needing to be wooed one more time.

If the location is desirable enough,
a male might attract multiple females.

The female makes a *check* sound,
when they are not doing anything
      except waiting.

The male makes a *tseer* warning sound

if you come too close. He is defiant
and defensive.

He makes a *teeteeteetee*
in a series of short, intense, high whistles
      whimpering,

    his call of courtship,
    his call for attention.

    These one-second sounds
     from the high branches
      lean forward,
     drop their wings,
    spread tail feathers,

All Beautiful Things Need Not Fly

fluff bright shoulder patches,
      showing off.

What part of this
does not represent
    what I did
when I first met you?

IV

All Beautiful Things Need Not Fly

The Mind is an Eraser

1.

mother takes me birdwatching

she teaches me how to focus
binoculars to identify birds
      by sound

she mostly prefers the black birds
they are harder to identify

2.

small black birds took off
      one
          after another

more birds broke silence
into shards of air

mother could hear them
tiny black berries at this distance

her heart misfiring cylinders
inquiring *what makes life*

3.

mother eats bird-like
pecking at rice

(as a child I fed an abandoned baby robin
      with an eye-dropper
         one squeeze and wait)

I feed my mother drop
    by missed drop
as she closes her beak

she forgets what a mouth is for

it expresses memory/
    lack of memory

4.

black birds move awkwardly fighting wind
    struggling like my mother

5.

wind off the Gulf Stream arrives different
Franklin gulls won't challenge those wind

the wind turns significantly strong enough
to make their black heads surrender

(the strongest current
comes from the one in the corridor
bringing gusts of silence
to my mother's mind)

6.

distance traveling between words becomes wider

it becomes increasingly impossible
    to fly against headwinds
no one takes off in these conditions

brown-headed cowbirds do not risk tiring their wings

    mother takes off

7.

in her mind she could be dancing
      in a large ballroom
         to music not there

 at the end is a dot of light
       her eyes track

     deadness inside

(a robin-sized rusty blackbird watches
       with its pale-yellow eyes
        making a *chack* song
like swinging a corroded gate hinge)

mother responds by turning towards the noise
   never having seen *this* bird before

9.

once a person slips into a hole
they escape to the other side
    as a musical note
from a red-winged blackbird
    a liquid burbling
       tee-err

10.

the mind furiously bails
its canoe from a slow leak
filling faster than buckets can toss
into an endless ocean

(a petite blackish head
Bonaparte's gull

circles above in the loss
makes a nasal *cherr*)

she has this bucket
with a gaping hole

11.

(an iridescent-black boat-tailed grackle scolds
in whistles

      clucks

      then harshly
      check

      check

      check)

12.

she had been staring at a mirror
      for days

   no one reflects there
     no one *home*

   a clean slate

(outside, swift speckled eastern starlings
    s c a t t e r   as wind
taking their whistled *whoooe* sound with them)

  the mirror darkens
shedding coal-black feathers

13.

disappearances come more often
lasting longer
are more profound
more pronounced

after a while
absence becomes permanent
the mind migrates elsewhere
into the *Nowhere*

she misplaces the names of objects
Where did I leave them this time?

(A large hawk-like northern raven alternates flapping
sailing on flat wings
croaking *cr-r-ruck*
with his "Roman-nose" beak)

mother alternates falling and swooping

14.

she squawks
do I know you?

(black birds tap on her window)

((a spirit guide?))

15.

when a drop of water lands on paper
    it leaves a fingerprint

mother becomes that drop
    leaving no trace

    black birds have left for the season
        not one snowflake stays

(think how long one drifting snowflake takes
        to fall from the sky

        how long her thoughts take
        sometimes never landing)

16.

    she had been sitting in the dark
        gazing into it
as if she was watching a television show

        I want to ask
        what she sees there

        but she was in so deep
        she had no turning back

17.

one day like any other day she went outside
    onto the porch
that is as far as she went

she stood all day in rain until someone moved her
    asking her what she was doing
she did not answer or blink or respond
    she had flown away
  left her body behind an empty nest
woven with twigs and white hair and twine

    they put her away
    for her own good
    for her own protection
this becomes when she began escaping

18.

dates and days
became important to her

I keep saying

    it is Wednesday
      it is noon

in a lucid moment
    she asks
when's the last time we went on a family vacation

    I'm guessing

      June
    fifty years ago

anything more precise I can't do

19.

(she has been dead over a year now)

I can't remember the date
    I could look it up
I have a death certificate

    I think

  I'm not certain
    I must be sure

20.

(I tried to build a purple martin house
with many round doors
like an apartment complex

      but none checked in
it fell apart as soon as one landed
      I was a bad builder
their rich *tchew-wew* laughed at me

what made me think I could repair her mind)

21.

after a while all she wore was pajamas
scuffling across the floor in slippers

she did not know where she was
      I'd answer
        home

            she'd ask
           where's that

      I'd respond
where the heart is

(momentary silence while she puzzled it out)

eventually I'd remind her
it's time for me to go

she would be curious and question
      who are you

she was not being metaphysical

22.

the quick wingbeats of a peregrine falcon
      its *kek, kek, kek*

23.

    I left her
I visited less and less
   I forgot to visit

months flocked away

black birds roosted in my heart
   blackening out memory

      and then

    she was gone

24.

she died in her sleep

simply slipped away
in a boat of silence

broken wings moving in pajamas
     her voice circling
       who are you

I do not have a good answer

It Is All Written in Celtic Woods

(The Druid Calendar has two versions; this is the one related to animals. The Druid calendar has thirteen months and has different times than traditional calendars.)

1. **Stag/Deer**
    Celtic Astrology, December 24 – January 20

This begins a good time to start a new project,
    just not the one we have in mind.
Winter moon lies low enough to be in snow.

Be persistent, the stag echoes, this is your birthright;
       time to buck past boundaries.

Integrity is your trademark, the deer promises.
    She watches the city envelope in snow,
streetlights shuddering, all traces being covered.

    These are all parts of your sign.

2. **Cat**
    Celtic Astrology, January 21 – February 17

Look at what the cat dragged in.
       She purrs,
dropping the mouse as an offering.
She easily bats mice around.

With the sixth-mental sense,
she could see trouble coming.
She could be creative about cruelty.

You are always on the fringe,
    observing reactions.

3.   **Snake**
       Celtic Astrology, February 18 – March 17

Always curious about how the world works,
        ready to take apart things
          to see their inner workings,
figuring the answers out, like logarithms,
          in your curious head.

       You break things down
to the essence, what remains? When you know
    all there is to know, what remains?
        Nothing is too microscopic.

Your sign finds the edge of breakthrough
    with one of the greatest mysteries,
after years of research, calculations, observations,
        pulling all-nighters.

4.   **Fox**
       Celtic Astrology, March 18 – April 14

You know how to work a room,
a sly smile just a hint of what is to come
if you are the lucky one.

Know how to make traps,
the scent of her red fur intoxicating.
      Slinky, curve
like light over a convex object.

Be all smoke and mirrors,
whispers of guile and pomegranate,
smart enough to use what she has,
clever enough to use it to your best advantage,
vigorous as a gymnastic
      fox
pouncing upon rabbits.

I saw a fox licking the back of her wrists
      with a satisfied,
  I-ate-the-whole-thing look.

5.   Bull
Celtic Astrology, April 15 – May 12

Your sign keeps you focusing on the bullseye.
      You paw the ground
before charging blindly towards mistakes.

Love intuition kicks in:
        I should have quit her,
        long time ago.

That old blues line, sharp as a twelve chord
      from "The Killing Floor."
    Some stampedes into love
  will simply be not worth it.

Howling Wolf sure did know
how some women kept on the prowl,
and sometimes you just got to *howl*
and *growl* at the moon
when they cross your path.

    I should add,
men can be on the prowl, too.

Your sign could spot a liar a mile away.

Don't put your tail between your legs,
snorting out the door,
shoulders grazing the door,
China dishes smashing behind you,
wondering what your ex-lover is doing now.

A bull knows the wide range of a pasture.

6. Seahorse
Celtic Astrology, May 13 – June 9

Your sign always finds a loophole,
some legal-out, some hocus-pocus slight-of-hand,
because you are flexible. Changeable as weather,
always with a cautious eye looking out
        for yourself.

Did it ever occur to you,
you can bend backwards, only so far,
before every problem catches up to you?

You think you are so loveable,
that no problem can affect you.

You are wrong; as wrong as wrong can be.

7. Wren
Celtic Astrology, June 10 – July 7

Sing sweet melodies enchanting your friends,
notes lilting into sunrise. You can calm
in storm-raging clouds and titter all day.
You know how to get what you want.
All you have to do is whistle.

The path clears before you, all dark shadows
        rub off onto someone else.
  You seek balance where there is none.
Cheerful, even when you have no right to be.

8. Horse
Celtic Astrology, July 8 – August 4

You are confident when you are wrong,
always had a strategy and a backup plan,

always know the quickest way out,
always roam on the edges, pacing.
Charming to a fault, almost flirting
to potential lovers, swaying the easily
on their haunches. If they get too close,
you flick and trot away.

9. **Salmon**
   Celtic Astrology, August 5 – September 1

You could dive into yourself, slow breathes
into stillness, on the edge of not breathing,
nothing flinching, almost never surfacing,

meditation becomes easy, as if you have gill slits,
            did not need oxygen.
You could surface as words on paper.

Some places you do not belong, where silence
becomes too close to not-being anymore,
disappearing into a black hole of your own making.

10. **Swan**
    Celtic Astrology, September 2 – September 29

Spiritually evolved, you could glide across,
a reflection of a red swan upon green waters,
feathers of glass awakening.

What appears to be detached is really attuned,
the movement of planets.

You can compose yourself, addressing any tiny flaws,
pruning here, decorating there,
an orchestra tuning up.

Float as a line of sight,
a command performance.

11.   Butterfly
Celtic Astrology, September 30 — October 27

You are everywhere, all at once, multi-tasking,
trying to fill the void, no matter how unimportant
and trivial. Always in air, dancing,
you cannot be still if your life depended on it.

If you were hurt in an accident,
you would administer your own cure.
You might even talk in your sleep.

12.   Wolf
Celtic Astrology, October 28 — November 24

This sign has a strong sense of purpose,
    a commission to undertake,

but no instructions how to proceed,
      no request to fulfill.

You will not back down,
    not heed.

You are always getting ready
    for something,

      uncertain
what you are preparing for.

Somewhere, wolves in the tundra
    knows this instinct.

You know where you stood with wolves:
either protected and belonging or prey.

13. Falcon/Hawk
Celtic Astrology, November 25 — December 23

Life all depends on interest.
Either swooping in;
or pass by, ignoring.

Decisions all depend on
a clearness of sight,
to see which is which,
and what is most vulnerable.

Carefulness depends
on knowledge,
how much to share,
whom to share it,
how much to be cautious.

Attach or not attack,
swoop or circle around
depends on too many factors.

Discernment is needed.

       Study first,
then, pick a logical course of action.

Many forms of hypothesis become necessary,

       but quickness must follow
         like shadow
         follows light.

Our Hearts Are Weighed When We Are Born

(Not all Zodiacs begin somewhere in December. Egyptians started with August.)

1. **Thoth (August 29 – September 27)**
   Thoth is the god of wisdom and learning,
   often portrayed with an Ibis head
              writing poetry or math.

You are good with critical thinking,
but your impatience creates more problems
for you to solve. Be less like the wind,
and more like the crocodiles, waiting patiently
before reacting irrationally.

Wisdom understands how to store knowledge,
like grain for the famine seasons.
You must learn from past mistakes;
then your ideas will flow like the Nile
where everyone benefits.

2. **Horus (September 28 – October 27)**
   Horus is god of the sky, portrayed with a falcon head.

You are a risk-taker. Sometimes, this becomes dangerous,
     making you stubborn and impractical.
You lack caution, like Ibis drinking near the Nile edge
        filled with crocodiles.

Like the chariot wheel, you are self-motivated
     to move forward through life.

    This is the sign of Pharaohs in life.

The sun in your right eye, the moon in your left,
you are always searching for new things to get.
     Restless heart always flying.

3.   Wadget (October 28 – November 26)
     Wadget is the goddess of the royal cobra.

Caution, they say, coils inside you.
Or it can strike blindly with opinionated ideas.
Rational and suspicious at the same time,
a striking personality.

Called *Lady of Flame,*
Wadget could spit poison
into the enemy. Be careful of spite.
Beware of your feelings of pessimism.
Beware of acting with intense suddenness.

4.   Sekhmet (November 27 – December 26)
     Sekhmet is the goddess of war and healing,
     portrayed as a lioness.

     Your sign means optimism.
     How can you be so certain?

You have imagination and an encyclopedia of interests.
What are you doing with these skills?

Are you putting them to good use?
Using them for arguing is not using your skills for good.

You are resilient; but how far can you bend backwards
when you naturally believe in good outcomes?

     Be careful of that hot temper;
flame can be extinguished eventually.

Can you heal what needs protecting?
Or will you tear apart the wounded with more vicious words?

It is never the lion who brings back the prey.
It is always the lioness.

5.   **Sphinx (December 27 – January 25)**
        Sphinx is the guardian, portrayed with
        a lion body,   large wings, and human head,
        seen as the Pyramid of Gaza.

Winter always riddles what will survive.
This makes you sensible and adaptable.

Because bad things can happen in darkness,
        you are on guard.
            Your eyes are low stars.

A lion knows how to wait.

            This is your riddle.
            The riddle of you:

What can make you take off? Why is the desert silent?
   What can be seen at a distance but not up close?
        Where is the beginning of the end?

6.   **Shu (January 26 – February 24)**
        Shu is the god of air,
        portrayed with ostrich feathers.

You are emptiness.

You should practice meditation.
but you are too busy trying to be successful,
you miss how unfulfilled your life really is.

You are afraid of failure,
making you hesitate like an ostrich.

Words are full of air.

What are you holding back?

Success should be measured differently,
    in small pieces
so you can see you are accomplishing things,

        otherwise,
        you cannot see
        what is not there.

Stop sticking your neck out for others;
    you're not an ostrich.

7.   **Isis (February 25 – March 25)**
    Isis is the goddess of discipline, nature, magic,
    friend to slaves and artists,
    portrayed with a throne on her head.

Your sign goes straightforward as sight,
as confident as an artist believing in their craft,
and as idealistic as a magician trying to raise the dead.

    You cannot sit for long,
or you will get lost in a labyrinth of thought
    created from the bones of slaves.

Discipline understands what true power is,
and it is not control, for thrones are only secure
    for a short time before lost;
    but a wise and kind ruler
    can live to see many harvests.
This is always something to think about.

8.   **Osiris (March 27 – April 25)**
    Osiris is the god of the underworld,
    depicted as a green-skinned man
    with a pharaoh's beard,
    partially mummy-wrapped at the legs,
    wearing a crown with two large ostrich feathers
    at each side and holding a symbolic crook and flail.

You are paradoxes within paradoxes,
        easily misunderstood.
Your words unwrap as mummy strips.

You shy away from your responsibilities,
trying to outrun them like an ostrich,
but sooner or later, you are tripped up by a crook
like an old vaudevillian comic with bad jokes
yanked off stage before the rotten tomatoes fly.

You have no need to flail yourself or others
       until faces turn green like frogs.
Misunderstandings are common as feathers.

   When we die, there is a long journey
and we must be ready, taking what we need
          to the next world,
whether it is a jar filled with internal organs,
or a poem as long as a pharaoh's beard.

9.   **Amun (April 20 – May 25)**
        Amun is the god of creation, a wind deity,
        whose plumes on his head
        are either ram horns or obelisks.

You are the wind and the long road ahead.
       are a natural leader,

       but you can be intolerant.
Be careful not to butt against others like a ram.

A strong will is all air and can be held back by any wall.
Your following can change direction like the wind.

Remember, Amenhotep IV disliked the temple power.
So, he moved the capital and weakened the temple.

Fortunes come and fortunes go,
but a ram can climb any cliff.

10. Hathor (May 26 – June 24)
Hathor is the goddess of love, music, dance,
women in childbirth, and miners, depicted as a cow
goddess with head horns in which is set a sun disk
with Uraeus, probably dating back
to the domestication of cows.

You are emotional,
   crying milk.
Your eyes tell me all about love,
   mining gold
while searching for new music.

Your feelings are all highs and extreme lows –
   the sun
   dancing with joy of new births,
     all day,

then, sleeping in a cave, nightly,
one eye watching grazing cattle
   for predators.

Such is love – old as time itself,
tranquil and domesticated.

11. Phoenix (June 25 – July 24)
Phoenix is the bird of life and resurrection.

To you, everything can be possible,
every day a resurrection, a hopeful
flexibility. This makes you dreamy,
smoldering like stirred ashes.

This makes you introverted, you so rise
out of yourself, forcing yourself to go out,
   seek others,

because possibilities can only occur
if you make them happen.

12. Anubis (July 25 – August 28)
Anubis is the guardian of the underworld,
jackal-headed, associated with mummification.

You have a great ability to control,
and the determination necessary to accomplish it.
You weigh my heart with an invisible scale,
determining my worthiness.

You would make a good mortician.
You need an uncaring attitude and numbness,
speaking for the dead.

Is my heart heavy?
Or does it weigh less than an ostrich feather?

All Beautiful Things Need Not Fly

Acknowledgments:

Autumn Sky Poetry Daily: "Deer Country"

Birdsong: "Perfect and Terrifying"

Bitterzoit: "Encounter," "Searching for What We Never Find"

Broadkill River Review: "Work Horse"

Califragile: "A Flamingo Always Has One Leg Up, Ready to Fly If It Needs To," "Reams of Light"

Comstock Review: "After a Rough Season," "A White Stitch"

Gyroscope Review: "The Elephants Sing About Everlasting Love"

Live Encounters: "Nothing is Perfectly Still"

Lothlorien Poetry Journal: "Why Cicadas Are Noisy"

New Verse News: "Shooting the Last Female White Giraffe"

Red Wolf Journal: "Departing," "When Geese Leave"

Turtle Island Quarterly: "Blue-Winged Darter (Dragonfly),"

"Four Blue Horses," "Sky Writing"

Verse-Virtual: "Transitioning"

"It Is All Written in Celtic Woods" appeared in the anthology, *What's Your Sign* (A Kind of Hurricane Press, 2013)

"The Mind Is an Eraser" appeared in the anthology, *Dementia*, Beatlick Press, 2019)

"Red-Winged Blackbirds" was a broadside Benevolent Bird Press, 2011)

"Released from My Heart" appeared in the anthology, *Tranquility* (A Kind of Hurricane Press, 2016)

Author Profile

Martin Willitts Jr is an editor of Comstock Review. He won 2014 Dylan Thomas International Poetry Contest; Stephen A. DiBiase Poetry Prize, 2018; Editor's Choice, Rattle Ekphrastic Challenge, December 2020; 17th Annual Sejong Writing Competition, 2022. His 21 full-length collections include the Blue Light Award 2019, "The Temporary World". His recent books are "Harvest Time" (Deerbrook Editions, 2021); "All Wars Are the Same War" (FutureCycle Press, 2022); "Not Only the Extraordinary are Exiting the Dream World (Flowstone Press, 2022); "Ethereal Flowers" (Shanti Arts Press, 2023); "Rain Followed Me Home" (Glass Lyre Press, 2023); and "Leaving Nothing Behind" (Fernwood Press, 2023). His forthcoming is "The Thirty-Six Views of Mount Fuji" including all 36 color pictures (Shanti Arts Press, 2024).

www.ingramcontent.com/pod-product-compliance
Lightning Source LLC
Chambersburg PA
CBHW071403080526
44587CB00017B/3170